CONNECT BIBLE STUDIES

A.I.

Dir. Stephen Spielberg
(Warner Bros., 2001)

Being Human
Negative Emotions
Ties that Bind
Hope

www.connectbiblestudies.com

connect
linking the Word to the world

CONNECT BIBLE STUDIES: A.I.

Published in this format by Scripture Union, 207-209 Queensway, Bletchley, MK2 2EB, England.

Scripture Union is an international Christian charity working with churches in more than 130 countries providing resources to bring the good news about Jesus Christ to children, young people and families — and to encourage them to develop spiritually through the Bible and prayer.

As well as a network of volunteers, staff and associates who run holidays, church-based events and school Christian groups, Scripture Union produces a wide range of publications and supports those who use the resources through training programmes.

Email: info@scriptureunion.org.uk
Internet: www.scriptureunion.org.uk

© Damaris Trust, PO Box 200, Southampton, SO17 2DL.

Damaris Trust enables people to relate Christian faith and contemporary culture. It helps them to think about the issues within society from a Christian perspective and to explore God's truth as it is revealed in the Bible. Damaris provides resources via the Internet, workshops, publications and products.

Email: office@damaris.org
Internet: www.damaris.org

ALSO AVAILABLE AS AN ELECTRONIC DOWNLOAD: www.connectbiblestudies.com

Chief editor: Nick Pollard
Consultant Editor: Andrew Clark
Managing Editor: Di Archer
Written by Di Archer, James Murkett, Caroline Puntis, Tony Watkins

First published 2001
ISBN 1 85999 624 4

British Library Cataloguing-in-Publication Data: a catalogue record for this book is available from the British Library.

Cover design and print production by:
CPO, Garcia Estate, Canterbury Road, Worthing, West Sussex BN13 1BW.

Other titles in this series:

Harry Potter and the Goblet of Fire ISBN 1 85999 578 0
The Matrix ISBN 1 85999 579 9
U2: All that you can't leave behind ISBN 1 85999 580 2
Billy Elliot ISBN 1 85999 581 0
Chocolat ISBN 1 85999 608 6
Game Shows ISBN 1 85999 609 4
How to be Good ISBN 1 85999 610 8
Destiny's Child: Survivor ISBN 1 85999 613 2

And more titles following — check www.connectbiblestudies.com for latest titles or ask at any good Christian bookshop.

Using Connect Bible Studies

What Are These Studies?

These innovative home group Bible studies have two aims. Firstly, we design them to enable group members to dig into their Bibles and get to know them better. Secondly, we aim to help members to think through topical issues in a Biblical way. Hence the studies are based on a current popular book or film etc. The issues raised by these are the subjects for the Bible studies.

We do not envisage that all members will always be able to watch the films or read the books, or indeed that they will always want to. A summary is always provided. However, our vision is that knowing about these films and books empowers Christians to engage with friends and colleagues about them. Addressing issues from a Biblical perspective gives Christians confidence that they know what they think, and can bring a distinctive angle to bear in conversations.

The studies are produced in sets of four — i.e. four weeks' worth of group Bible Study material. These are available in print published by Scripture Union from your local Christian bookshop, or via the Internet at www.connectbiblestudies.com. Anyone can sign up for a free monthly email newsletter that announces the new studies and provides other information (sign up on the Connect Bible Studies website at www.connectbiblestudies.com/uk/register).

How Do I Use Them?

We design the studies to stimulate creative thought and discussion within a Biblical context. Each section therefore has a range of questions or options from which you as leader may choose in order to tailor the study to your group's needs and desires. Different approaches may appeal at different times, so the studies aim to supply lots of choice. Whilst adhering to the main aim of corporate Bible study, some types of questions may enable this for your group better than others — so take your pick.

Group members should be supplied with the appropriate sheet that they can fill in, each one also showing the relevant summary.

Leader's notes contain:

1. Opening Questions

These help your group settle in to discussion, whilst introducing the topics. They may be straightforward, personal or creative, but are aiming to provoke a response.

2. Summary

We suggest the summary of the book or film will follow now, read aloud if necessary. There may well be reactions that group members want to express even before getting on to the week's issue.

3. Key Issue

Again, either read from the leader's notes, or summarised.

4. Bible Study

Lots of choice here. Choose as appropriate to suit your group — get digging into the Bible. Background reading and texts for further help and study are suggested, but please use the material provided to inspire your group to explore their Bibles as much as possible. A concordance might be a handy standby for looking things up. A commentary could be useful too, such as the *New Bible Commentary 21st century edition* (IVP, 1994). The idea is to help people to engage with the truth of God's word, wrestling with it if necessary but making it their own.

Don't plan to work through every question here. Within each section the two questions explore roughly the same ground but from different angles or in different ways. Our advice is to take one question from each section. The questions are open-ended so each ought to yield good discussion — though of course any discussion in a Bible study may need prompting to go a little further.

5. Implications

Here the aim is to tie together the perspectives gained through Bible study and the impact of the book or film. The implications may be personal, a change in worldview, or new ideas for relating to non-churchgoers. Choose questions that adapt to the flow of the discussion.

6. Prayer

Leave time for it! We suggest a time of open prayer, or praying in pairs if the group would prefer. Encourage your members to focus on issues from your study that had a particular impact on them. Try different approaches to prayer — light a candle, say a prayer each, write prayers down, play quiet worship music — aim to facilitate everyone to relate to God.

7. Background Reading

You will find links to some background reading on the Connect Bible Studies website: www.connectbiblestudies.com/

8. Online Discussion

You can discuss the studies online with others on the Connect Bible Studies website at www.connectbiblestudies.com/discuss/

www.connectbiblestudies.com

connect
linking the Word to the world

A. I.

Dir. Steven Spielberg (Warner Bros., 2001)

Part One: Being Human

He never makes the complete leap, but he progresses in the film to being more human.
Haley Joel Osment about playing David

Please read Using Connect Bible Studies *before leading a Bible study using this material.*

Opening Questions

Choose one of these questions.

What is the favourite machine in your life and why?	Did your favourite toy have a name? Why did you want to give it a name?
If you had been Pinocchio, why would you have wanted to be a 'real boy'?	Which inanimate object would you like to come 'alive' and why?

Summary

It is some time in the future and Artificial Intelligence has become part of everyday life. All kinds of machines, known as 'mechas', have been created to fulfil the insatiable needs of the human race. Every mecha understands that its purpose is to serve humans. For example, the 'lover mecha' has been built to satisfy humans sexually. Although these sophisticated robots have the outward appearance of humans ('orgas') and can simulate emotions by copying, they are not yet able to respond emotionally themselves. They are not able to actually love. Professor Hobby's latest project is to develop artificial intelligence that will be able to experience the full range of human emotions. He has created the first mecha child whose purpose is to love. His name is David.

David is given for testing to a couple grieving over their own son who is in a coma and not expected to recover. When Monica reads a special code to him, David's ability to love her is activated. His whole existence begins to revolve around the subject of his new mother, but can Monica ever really love him back? David knows that he is not human. When he hears the story of Pinocchio, David becomes obsessed with the idea that he too could be made into a real boy. Long after the human race has disappeared from earth, advanced robots recreate Monica for just one day to make David happy. She finally tells him that she loves him and David falls asleep for the first time to dream his first dream. Has he become a real boy after all?

Key Issue: What does it mean to be human?

Stanley Kubrick, the driving force behind the film *AI — Artificial Intelligence* — cannot be the only one fascinated by the thought of how far our invention of technology can go. Will there indeed come a day when we can create robots with feelings, like David in the film? Is the capacity to feel really all that separates us from our inventions? Do emotions keep us from being mere machines? *AI* explores the implications of what it means to be human, and whether a machine with feelings qualifies as a real boy or not. For Christians, the basic premise that we are created in the image of God is vital here. Our whole understanding of humanity flows from this belief. So in this opening study on the issues raised by *AI*, we tackle what the Bible says about the difference this makes. What does it mean to be human, made in the image of God?

Bible Study

Choose one question from each section.

1.   To love and be loved

But in the beginning, didn't God create Adam to love him? (Professor Hobby)

♦   Read Mark 12:28–34. What is said about the depth of love that God and other people deserve?

♦   Read 1 John 4:7–21. What is love all about?

2.   To have free will

The walk was always a repeat of itself. He never walks in a different way. There's a kind of limit within his freedom. It's a rather odd paradox. (Jude Law about playing Gigolo Joe)

♦   Read Joshua 24:14–27. What does Joshua ask the Israelites to do? Why does he choose not to renew the covenant after their first response?

Leaders: Joshua is issuing his last instructions to Israel before he dies. He assembles all the tribes and reminds them of all God has done for them before issuing them this challenge.

♦ Read Romans 3:9–20. Why is the world as it is? Where does this leave people in relation to God?

Leaders: Paul has defended the power of the gospel for salvation and gone on to show how both Gentiles and Jews alike have fallen short of God's standards.

3. To be unique

David: ***I thought I was one of a kind.***
Professor Hobby: ***My own son was one of a kind. You're the first of a kind.***

♦ Read Psalm 139:13–18. What is special about God's knowledge of us? How does this affect the Psalmist's perception of himself?

♦ 1 Corinthians 12:1–11. What does the fact that we are all different say about God? How does the Spirit affirm us as unique individuals?

4. To be spiritual

Love will be the key by which they acquire a subconscious ... of dreams. (Professor Hobby)

♦ Read John 3:1–15. What does Jesus say about our relationship to the kingdom of God? What are the implications of being 'born again'?

♦ Read 1 Corinthians 2:6–16. What does it mean to be spiritual? How does spiritual wisdom differ from 'the wisdom of this age'?

Implications

I propose that we build a robot who can love. (Professor Hobby)

Choose one or more of the following questions.

♦ Why do you think that Jesus said that to love God and to love our neighbours as ourselves are the greatest commandments? What does it mean for you?

♦ How are you expressing your individuality as a unique child of God, while still building community with others?

♦ How does choosing God's way work out in your daily life?

♦ Would you call yourself a 'born-again Christian'? Why, or why not?

♦ How would you explain 'eternal life' to a friend who thinks that life ends at death and that's OK?

♦ What would you say to a friend who argues that people are just a mixture of molecules?

♦ How do you respond to Jesus' saving you?

Prayer

Spend some time praying through these issues.

Background Reading

You will find links to some background reading on the Connect Bible Studies website: www.connectbiblestudies.com/uk/catalogue/0009/background.htm

Discuss

Discuss this study in the online discussion forums at www.connectbiblestudies.com/discuss

Members' Sheet: AI — Part 1

Summary

It is some time in the future and Artificial Intelligence has become part of everyday life. All kinds of machines, known as 'mechas', have been created to fulfil the insatiable needs of the human race. Every mecha understands that its purpose is to serve humans. For example, the 'lover mecha' has been built to satisfy humans sexually. Although these sophisticated robots have the outward appearance of humans and can simulate emotions by copying, they are not yet able to respond emotionally themselves. They are not able to actually love. Professor Hobby's latest project is to develop artificial intelligence that will be able to experience the full range of human emotions. He has created the first mecha child whose purpose is to love. His name is David.

David is given for testing to a couple grieving over their own son who is in a coma and not expected to recover. When Monica reads a special code to him, David's ability to love her is activated. His whole existence begins to revolve around the subject of his new mother, but can Monica ever really love him back? David knows that he is not human. When he hears the story of Pincocchio, David becomes obsessed with the idea that he too could be made into a real boy. Long after the human race has disappeared from earth, advanced robots recreate Monica for one day to make David happy. She finally tells him that she loves him and David falls asleep for the first time to dream his first dream. Has he become a real boy after all?

Key Issue

Bible Study notes

Implications

Prayer

connect

linking the Word to the world

A. I.

Dir. Steven Spielberg (Warner Bros., 2001)

Part Two: Negative Emotions

Dave is capable of love, hate, fear, jealousy and murder.
Review in *Rolling Stone* magazine, 19 July 2001

Please read Using Connect Bible Studies *before leading a Bible study using this material.*

Opening Questions

Choose one of these questions.

Did you respond emotionally to David in *AI*? Why/why not?	Do you think love and hate are 'two sides of the same coin'? Why/why not?
How would you define negative emotions?	Did you like the film *AI*? Why/why not?

Summary

Despite misgivings about the morality of the idea, Professor Hobby and his team embark on a project to create a child robot capable of loving. David is the result—a young prototype robot built to love one person. Though initially cautious, Monica Swinton — whose own son, Martin, is on a life-support machine and not expected to survive — takes him on as an experiment, and is quickly seduced by the prospect of having a child again, and being loved unconditionally. She activates his programme, which conditions him to love her.

Unfortunately for David, the flip side of his love for Monica is pain. David will never die; Monica is unlikely to live for more than fifty years. Since David has only been programmed to love one person forever, he realises that most of his existence will be full of the pain of loss. Consequently he starts to feel unwelcome emotions like worry and fear.

Then Martin makes a remarkable and unexpected recovery, and returns to the family home to find David there. Martin is jealous of David, and provokes him into various escapades which frighten Monica. Martin's hatred grows, and David then experiences fear as he is exposed to threat and challenge. Desperation and despair set in as David is turned out of the home and left to fend for himself, with only his loyal robot teddy as company. He encounters a cold, hard world which scares him, but finds a friend in Gigolo Joe who helps him in his search to become a real boy and thus be lovable again to Monica.

Key Issue: Negative emotions

AI explores the idea that what makes us human is the ability to feel emotions. David the robot is a big experiment — what difference will it make that he is programmed to feel, and specifically to love? Poor David finds he is in for a rough ride, as his capacity to love catapults him into a world without it. His main experience of emotions therefore is fairly negative. So how do we deal with painful emotions, as real human beings? Does the Bible acknowledge these emotions, or help us to cope with them? How are hatred, jealousy, despair and fear portrayed?

Bible Study

Choose one question from each section. You may want to follow the Genesis questions throughout this section.

1. **Hate**

    If he was created to love, it is reasonable to assume that he knows how to hate. (Harry Swinton)

    ◆   Read Genesis 37:1–8. How would you account for the tension between Joseph and his brothers? Why did the dream make things worse?

    ◆   1 John 2:1–11. Why does hatred leave us in darkness? How do we walk in the light?

2. **Jealousy**

    I guess you're the new supertoy. Can you do power stuff like walk on walls? (Martin)

    ◆   Read Genesis 37:9–36. What effect did the dreams have on the whole family's feelings? Describe the resulting chain of events.

    ◆   Read Acts 13:42–52. Why were the Jews jealous? What effect did their jealousy have on the spread of the Gospel?

3. Despair

I'm sorry I didn't tell you about the world (Monica Swinton)

- ◆ Read Genesis 42:17–38. Why do the brothers and Jacob despair? How did Joseph's intervention expose their feelings about the past?

  Leaders: Joseph had been taken to Egypt where he gained prominence serving in Potiphar's house. He was falsely accused of seducing Potiphar's wife and thrown into prison. After several years he was released after interpreting a dream for Pharaoh. Pharaoh made Joseph his highest official. Joseph's brothers arrived in Egypt as there was a famine in the area and only Egypt had any food.

- ◆ Read Acts 27:13–20. How did the sailors attempt to avoid despair? What did despair mean for them?

4. Fear

David, you won't understand the reasons, but I have to leave you here. (Monica to David)

- ◆ Read Genesis 43:1–23. Why were the brothers afraid? How did Joseph respond to their vulnerability?

- ◆ Read Luke 12:4–7. How does Jesus challenge our understanding of fear? Why do we not need to be afraid?

Implications

When will you come back for me? (David to Monica when she abandons him)

Choose one or more of the following questions.

♦ Have you experienced sibling rivalry, and are there any outstanding issues that need dealing with?

♦ Do you often find yourself reacting negatively to family members? How can you change this?

♦ How, in practical terms, does our security in God set us free from fear?

♦ Which of the difficult emotions identified today do you relate to most? How can you let God help you with this?

♦ Do you agree with *AI*'s idea that the ability to feel emotions makes us human? Does this have any bearing on the argument for the existence of a creator God?

♦ Are you in a situation about which you feel despair? Can you let the group help and pray for you?

Prayer

Spend some time praying through these issues.

Background Reading

You will find links to some background reading on the Connect Bible Studies website: www.connectbiblestudies.com/uk/catalogue/0009/background.htm

Discuss

Discuss this study in the online discussion forums at www.connectbiblestudies.com/discuss

Members' Sheet: AI — Part 2

Summary

Despite misgivings about the morality of the idea, Professor Hobby and his team embark on a project to create a child robot capable of loving. David is the result—a young prototype robot built to love one person. Though initially cautious, Monica Swinton — whose own son, Martin, is on a life-support machine and not expected to survive — takes him on as an experiment, and is quickly seduced by the prospect of having a child again, and being loved unconditionally. She activates his programme, which conditions him to love her.

Unfortunately for David, the flip side of his love for Monica is pain. David will never die; Monica is unlikely to live for more than fifty years. Since David has only been programmed to love one person forever, he realises that most of his existence will be full of the pain of loss. Consequently he starts to feel unwelcome emotions like worry and fear.

Then Martin makes a remarkable and unexpected recovery, and returns to the family home to find David there. Martin is jealous of David, and provokes him into various escapades which frighten Monica. Martin's hatred grows, and David then experiences fear as he is exposed to threat and challenge. Desperation and despair set in as David is turned out of the home and left to fend for himself, with only his loyal robot teddy as company. He encounters a cold, hard world which scares him, but finds a friend in Gigolo Joe who helps him in his search to become a real boy and thus be lovable again to Monica.

Key Issue

Bible Study notes

Implications

Prayer

A. I.

Dir. Steven Spielberg (Warner Bros., 2001)

Part Three: Ties that Bind

She loves what you do for her
Gigolo Joe about Monica

Please read Using Connect Bible Studies *before leading a Bible study using this material.*

Opening Questions

Choose one of these questions.

How would your life be different if you didn't have children?	How would your life be different if you did have children?
What do you think about the trade in children from abroad, eg China to the West?	Could a robot programmed to love ever really be a substitute for a child? Why?

Summary

In the future world of the Swintons, life seems bleak. The law permits every couple to have only one child — and their son Martin is as good as dead. In desperation, Monica goes to visit Martin every day at the centre where he lies frozen in a cryogenics tank. She reads to him through the glass, hoping that one day he will come back to life and be part of the family once again.

Meanwhile, Professor Hobby—who has lost his own son—and the cryogenics company have manufactured a prototype robot called David. He is a child who can be programmed to love one specific person. The Swintons are selected for the testing process. In agreeing, Henry Swinton hopes that family life can be restored to his unhappy home. Though at first reluctant, Monica begins to warm to the robot child, so desperate is she to give and receive love as a mother again.

Confusion ensues when Martin recovers and ousts David from his mother's affection and the family home. David's existence turns into a frantic search for the Blue Fairy of Pinocchio fame, believing she can turn him into a real boy whom Monica will love again. However, it is Professor Hobby who greets David at the end of the trail. The Professor is delighted at the success of his experiment—he has created a feeling, emotionally-driven robot, so he can now provide loving robot-children to order.

Key Issue: Ties That Bind

In this study we look at the sensitive issue of those who long for children, either because they have lost them — like Professor Hobby and Monica of *AI* — or because they are not able to have any. This is not an easy subject, so how can God's Word help us? Does it recommend family life? Does it recognise those consuming feelings of longing or grief? Will it aid us in our struggle to deal with these overwhelming emotions, and give us a way ahead?

Bible Study

Choose one question from each section.

1. ### When you wish upon a star ...

    'At last — a love of your own' (Slogan on 'David' box)

    ♦   Read 1 Samuel 1:1–20. How did Hannah show the depth of her feelings? How helpful were others' reactions to her anguish?

    ♦   Read Luke 8:40–56. How did Jairus demonstrate how he felt about his daughter? What was Jesus' response to the two daughters in these verses?

2. ### Why do we have family?

    Henry: *He's only a child ... Monica, he's a toy.*
    Monica: *He's a gift.*

    ♦   Read Psalm 78:1–8. What reasons does the Psalmist give for family? Why are they important?

    ♦   Read John 19:25–27. What does Jesus want John to do for his mother? What does the context of Jesus' request tell us about his attitude to family?

3.   When it doesn't work out …

I'll be alone. (David upon realising that Monica will one day die)

♦   Read Judges 11:29–40. Why was this such a tragedy for father and daughter? What does it say about promises to God?

Leaders: The Ammonites were attacking Israel, and Jephthah the warrior had been asked to lead the defence. Making vows was a common practice among the Israelites, and the story implies that this vow resulted in Jephthah offering his daughter as a sacrifice. That his daughter would therefore never marry or bear children was a great grief, as this was what daughters were brought up to do.

♦   Read Matthew 2:13–18. What were the boys — and their mothers — the victims of? How was what happened part of bigger events?

4.   Desires of our hearts?

I can't accept this. There is no substitute for your own child. (Monica to Henry upon David's arrival.)

♦   Read Psalm 145:13b–21. What does this Psalm promise? Who qualifies for these promises?

♦   Read Philippians 4:10–19. What is Paul's secret? How does he respond to those who support him in his times of need?

Implications

Monica recites the words on his imprinting card that will make Dave love her for life.
Should Monica tire of her mecha son, there is no deprogramming card. (Review in *Rolling Stone* magazine, 19 July 2001)

Choose one or more of the following questions.

- How do we deal with unfulfilled longings?

- How can we support those who long for children but cannot have them, for whatever reason?

- Both Monica and Professor Hobby try to replace lost children with David the robot. What healthier ways are there to bring comfort to bereaved parents, or those without children?

- How can we learn to be content, whatever our circumstances?

- What do you think family is for?

- Is there a point when the longing for children can tip over into treating them as consumer items, and if so, where is it?

- What would you say to someone who blames God for their lack of family?

Prayer

Spend some time praying through these issues.

Background Reading

You will find links to some background reading on the Connect Bible Studies website: www.connectbiblestudies.com/uk/catalogue/0009/background.htm

Discuss

Discuss this study in the online discussion forums at www.connectbiblestudies.com/discuss

Members' Sheet: AI — Part 3

Summary

In the future world of the Swintons, life seems bleak. The law permits every couple to have only one child — and their son Martin is as good as dead. In desperation, Monica goes to visit Martin every day at the centre where he lies frozen in a cryogenics tank. She reads to him through the glass, hoping that one day he will come back to life and be part of the family once again.

Meanwhile, Professor Hobby—who has lost his own son—and the cryogenics company have manufactured a prototype robot called David. He is a child who can be programmed to love one specific person. The Swintons are selected for the testing process. In agreeing, Henry Swinton hopes that family life can be restored to his unhappy home. Though at first reluctant, Monica begins to warm to the robot child, so desperate is she to give and receive love as a mother again.

Confusion ensues when Martin recovers and ousts David from his mother's affection and the family home. David's existence turns into a frantic search for the Blue Fairy of Pinocchio fame, believing she can turn him into a real boy whom Monica will love again. However, it is Professor Hobby who greets David at the end of the trail. The Professor is delighted at the success of his experiment—he has created a feeling, emotionally-driven robot, so he can now provide loving robot-children to order.

Key Issue

Bible Study notes

Implications

Prayer

connect

linking the Word to the world

A. I.

Dir. Steven Spielberg (Warner Bros., 2001)

Part Four: Hope

Only orga believe what cannot be seen or measured
Gigolo Joe ('orga' are real, organic people as opposed to 'mecha' robots)

Please read Using Connect Bible Studies *before leading a Bible study using this material.*

Opening Questions

Choose one of these questions.

Are you more likely to see problems or possibilities in a difficult situation? Why?	What did you hope for when you were a child?
Can people live without hope?	What do you think most people hope for?

Summary

When the robot child David is given to the Swintons, whose son is terminally ill, it is as if hope has been reborn. David is programmed to love Monica with the unswerving commitment of a child. His one hope is simply that Monica will love him back. However, the cryogenically frozen son returns to the family having been brought back to health. David's chance of being loved like a real son is ruined. Following a series of incidents, the Swintons decide to abandon David to the world outside and resume their cosy life.

Alone, David can only think about finding his mother again. He remembers her telling him the story of Pinocchio and becomes convinced that if he can only find the Blue Fairy, she will turn him into a real boy, just like Pinocchio. Then Monica will love him.

David's search leads him right back to his creator, Professor Hobby. The professor had been hoping all along that through his emotional experiences, David would learn to dream and hope. He is delighted — David, however, is devastated to realise that he is merely the first in a long production line of 'Davids'. He jumps into the sea and falls into the submerged ruins of the Coney Island theme park. There, David sees a statue of the Blue Fairy and thinks she is real. He starts to hope once again. Unfrozen 2,000 years later, his hope seems to be fulfilled. Superior robots find David, and recreate a loving Monica for him, just for a day.

Key Issue: Hope

In *AI*, Monica put her hope in a robot, while David put his in the Blue Fairy to make him into a real boy. This hope kept David going and inspired him on his perilous journeys. Hope is so important to us all, for without it there is only despair. We put our hope in many different things and people, some of which prove to be unworthy. This study takes a look at what the Bible says about hope. Is there a hope that can guarantee not to let us down? What can we hope for and how will those hopes affect us as we live our lives from day to day? What promises does the Bible really give us about the future?

Bible Study

Choose one question from each section. In this study, you may wish to follow the passages on either Ephesians or Revelation all the way through.

1.   What in? — God or self

The Blue Fairy is part of the great human flaw — that is to chase things that don't exist. (Professor Hobby)

◆   Read Ephesians 1:1–14. What does it mean to be a saint? How is hope guaranteed?

Leaders: Try not to get into lengthy discussions about predestination! There are different approaches on this subject, and our purpose here is to concentrate on hope.

◆   Read Revelation 1:9–20. Why does Jesus' appearance inspire fear in John? How would where Jesus is standing give John reason to hope?

Leaders: John, in exile on Patmos, writes to the seven churches to encourage them in a time of persecution. He sees a glorious vision of the risen Christ. There are echoes here of Daniel 7:9–14. Jesus is dressed in a robe and sash indicating his priestly ministry for us (Exodus 28:1–5). His hair and head indicate his divine status (Daniel 7), and possibly refer to wisdom and dignity (Proverbs 16:31). Jesus' eyes signify his insight, his feet his strength and stability (compare with Daniel 2:33, 40–43) and his voice a unique authority. His mouth indicates the thrust of his Word (Hebrews 4:12) and his face reflects his majesty (Matthew 17:2).

2. What for? — strength for today

... [David's] obsession (in Kubrick's terms) or dream (in Spielberg's) requires him to do everything to achieve Monica's love — after she renounces him, after she abandons him, after she's gone. (Review in *Time* magazine, 17 June 2001)

♦ Read Ephesians 1:15–23. What does Paul pray for, and why? How does his prayer encourage hope?

♦ Read Revelation 2:8–11. Why was the church in Smyrna in trouble? How does Jesus encourage the people?

Leaders: The synagogue of Satan probably refers to Jews who were revealing the whereabouts of Christians to the persecuting Roman officials. Ten days refers to a period of suffering that would come to an end, unlike God's eternal rule. The second death is referred to in Revelation 21:8.

3. Something that lasts — bright hope for tomorrow

... aspiration [comes] into play when David hears the story of Pinocchio and longs to become a real boy so that his mommy will love him as much as Martin. (N-Zone web site review)

♦ Read Ephesians 2:1–10. What does it mean to be saved? How does grace give us a future?

♦ Read Revelation 21:1–14. How will the future be different to what we know now? What will characterise the New Jerusalem? What is the cost?

Leaders: The New Jerusalem is symbolic of the fulfilment of all the Old and New Covenants, and of the consummation of God's kingdom. It represents both a people and a place — the bride-city (Revelation 21:2; 9–10 see also Ephesians 5:22–33). There are echoes here of Isaiah 55 and also Isaiah 65:17–25.

4. How does it affect you? — motivation

David and Teddy go on an incredible journey ... in their search for The Blue Fairy that David believes will make him a real boy. (N-Zone web site review)

♦ Read Ephesians 1:1–2:10. How does Paul challenge his readers with these words? What is his vision for hope in the life of a believer?

Leaders: If you have looked at parts of Ephesians 1:1–2:10 in the previous sections of this Bible study, please take time at this point to read through the whole passage again.

♦ Read Revelation 22:1–21. What were John's responses to the revelation he received? How did he expect his readers to react?

Implications

Please make me into a real live boy. (David to Blue Fairy)

Choose one or more of the following questions.

- What is your reaction to the vision of Jesus in Revelation 1?

- What impact does the message of Revelation have on how we live our lives today?

- 'We don't realise that Jesus is all we need until Jesus is all we have.' How true is that for you?

- How much do you allow your relationship with Jesus to impact your daily decisions?

- What do you understand about your hope for the future with Christ, and how would you explain it to a friend?

- If life is not working out for you how you wanted, how can you set your hope in God nevertheless?

- What would you say to a friend who maintains that there is no hope for the human race?

Prayer

Spend some time praying through these issues.

Background Reading

You will find links to some background reading on the Connect Bible Studies website: www.connectbiblestudies.com/uk/catalogue/0009/background.htm

Discuss

Discuss this study in the online discussion forums at www.connectbiblestudies.com/discuss

Members' Sheet: AI — Part 4

Summary

When the robot child David is given to the Swintons, whose son is terminally ill, it is as if hope has been reborn. David is programmed to love Monica with the unswerving commitment of a child. His one hope is simply that Monica will love him back. However, the cryogenically frozen son returns to the family having been brought back to health. David's chance of being loved like a real son is ruined. Following a series of incidents, the Swintons decide to abandon David to the world outside and resume their cosy life.

Alone, David can only think about finding his mother again. He remembers her telling him the story of Pinocchio and becomes convinced that if he can only find the Blue Fairy, she will turn him into a real boy, just like Pinocchio. Then Monica will love him.

David's search leads him right back to his creator, Professor Hobby. The professor had been hoping all along that through his emotional experiences, David would learn to dream and hope. He is delighted — David, however, is devastated to realise that he is merely the first in a long production line of 'Davids'. He jumps into the sea and falls into the submerged ruins of the Coney Island theme park. There, David sees a statue of the Blue Fairy and thinks she is real. He starts to hope once again. Unfrozen 2,000 years later, his hope seems to be fulfilled. Superior robots find David, and recreate a loving Monica for him, just for a day.

Key Issue

Bible Study notes

Implications

Prayer